MORBIDITY & ORNAMENT

MORBIDITY
&
ORNAMENT

Poems

Steve Noyes

OOLICHAN BOOKS
LANTZVILLE, BRITISH COLUMBIA, CANADA
2009

Library and Archives Canada Cataloguing in Publication

Noyes, Steve
Morbidity and ornament / Steve Noyes.

Poems.
ISBN 978-0-88982-260-3

I. Title.

PS8577.O96M67 2009   C811'.54   C2009-904762-4

We gratefully acknowledge the financial support of the Canada Council for the Arts, the British Columbia Arts Council through the BC Ministry of Tourism, Culture, and the Arts, and the Government of Canada through the Book Publishing Industry Development Program, for our publishing activities.

Published by
Oolichan Books
P.O. Box 10, Lantzville
British Columbia, Canada
V0R 2H0

Printed in Canada

"I move past the scaffolding and walk down the steps, hearing one language after another, rich, harsh, mysterious, strong. This is what we bring to the temple, not prayer or chant or slaughtered rams. Our offering is language."

—Don DeLillo

For Catherine and Miranda

CONTENTS

Tombs Arranged on Sloping Ground
Path / 13
The Man from 'Ad / 15
Daughter, Planetarium / 18
Anxiety Dream 1 / 19

Bats Become Mortal Fly
Prairie Lookout / 23
An Introduction to Chaucer / 25
Tracy Regetnig / 27
Gymnastics / 28
Frame / 30
Veneration / 32
Midwinter by the Dryer-Vent / 33

Pond-side a Marvelous Sis and Her Flute
Poutine with Comet / 37
The Kind / 39
Cigarette Humours / 41
One Day at a Time / 48
Anxiety Dream 3 / 49

The Lake Rat Swims Past
Catherine's Eyes / 53
Cow TV / 55
Shrew / 57
Ulterior Sheep / 58
Slugs, Mating / 60
Owl and the Unborn / 62
A Poem for Ramadan / 63

You and I Found a Small Stone
Living with the Lama / 67
Bodhisattva / 68
Basketball Anecdotes / 70
On First Looking into Allen Iverson / 75
The Blossoms of Chang'an / 76

Thought I Saw a Wolf
The Road to Ponteilla / 81
Meanwhile Evidence of Admiral Zheng He's 1421-23
   Expedition to North America Continues to
   Accumulate / 82
Canzone for Foreign Experts / 83
Qingdao's "Angry Youth" Flirt with a Rococo "International
   Style" while Holding Out for Supremacy / 86
Subjunctive Mood on Hainan Island / 88
O Little Town of Hankou / 90
The Shandong Dead / 92

Wrecked Houses in a Row
Career Path / 97
Iman / 99
Incarnation / 101
Empty Temple / 104

Fall, We Climb the Mountain
The Humans / 107
Aquino / 108
The Library at Alexandria / 111
As Was / 113

登原安排斜地上
蓝海软云下午梦
湿石而诮说幸福
有时远祖看心中

Deng yuan an pai xie di shang
Lan hai ruan yun xia wu meng
Shi shi er qiao shuo xing fu
You shi yuan zhu kan xin zhong

Tombs arranged on sloping ground
Blue sea soft clouds dreamy afternoon
Wet rocks whispered happiness
—The dead could see your heart.

PATH

These past days hauntings of a face, insistent.
Perhaps he saw me come in—
the mosque was crowded, a November day.
Rainy, the damp smell on everybody's clothes
as they finished in stretches their obligatory prayers
and folded legs, awaiting the *khutba*—
Perhaps he watched me assess the space and dip
downstairs, past the Arabic sign
hold fast to God, the most trustworthy handhold,

where I made my prayers, touching my forehead
to the ground, and squatted, shifting
often as I was not used to the sitting.
Sheets had been pinned to beams to enfold
a harem, the microphone's preparatory
screeches, then the raucous *khutba*—
And much else I have forgotten.

The bearded, incarnadine faces
tend to swim together in memory, the eyes
not hold me. When I came up the stairs
he was comfortably arranged in a corner,
one hand to the carpet, the other beckoning.
And I sat with him and we exchanged
the time-fresh greetings, *salaam aleykum,*
he fingering his beads,
assessing me from a distant place

far within his eyes, through veils of sophistication.
He let me know a little bit about himself.
I studied his *shalwar kameez,* his turban.
His children were in Algeria, in France,
for reasons of their education. And what
was he doing in Vancouver? He had affairs
to attend to. He pinched and slid his beads.

Of course, if one arranges one's responsibilities,
he smiled and let his look draw me
slightly forward, one can then travel
in the path of Allah. His eyes not unkind,
our conversation halted at a gate
as it were, with my question,
And what does one do in the path
of Allah?

Oh, there are many things in the path of Allah—
he smiled again, and repositioned himself.
If you had the time I would have asked
you for dinner, and he wished God's care
on me, and drew his robes together
and departed.

THE MAN FROM 'AD

Wa tilka 'Adun jahadu bi'ayati rabbihim
"Such were the 'Ad people
who rejected the signs of their Lord."
Qur'an, The Prophet Hud, 59.

Season of airports, their vaulted grey spaces,
drug-slow conveyors of vertical blood.
Awaiting transference, our skulls conduct
smooth international voices, we peer
at the monitors, arrivals, departures.
In the tedious torpor of wanting to move
and dead-time, he came out of nowhere,
touching my wrist, the man from 'Ad.
We salaamed each other. His one eye

had swallowed hope, the other, home.
He spoke in an effortful whisper and smelled
of deodorant-cubes in public washrooms;
he wore a many-layered newspaper robe.
His cheek bore the tattooed map-scallop
of an obscure shore. This in Seattle, Toronto,
Frankfurt, Chicago, some node in the flow.
A small negro child, with a high choker
of dried seeds around her throat, barefoot
and big-eyed, glided silent beside him.

She held his hand and would not let go.
We sat on high stools at the windows
overlooking the runway. He sniffed at his
sandwich, through the cellophane, once.
His free hand skimmed the table as he spoke.

"There was a wall of sand that stretched
to the heavens and rushed at us, thunderous,
the sun a dim smudge. Though we had
often heard the warning, many tried to run—
they were lifted and churned under, their legs
and arms splayed in starfish arrangement,

buried layer on layer. The tallest of the
tallest roofs poked out. Thus did our Lord
deal with 'Ad and its transgressions. I found
her peerless on the sand, and we began to roam."
The little girl's eyes were wide in opiate
of timeless silence. I grabbed his hand:
"You've told me this before," I cried,
"in Narita, in Heathrow, in JFK. Won't you
give it a break? Look around—there's no
catastrophe. The people come and go."
He chucked her chin, and the little girl
began to wolf the sandwich. He muttered low,

"The oceans and the sky are deeps divided
by a tenuous membrane; the towering rocks
mere crystals in a hidden watch. Have you not
seen the enormous pulse behind the forks
of lightning? We live at the behest of wind
and spinning ornaments. We come to warn
through ports of tattered sails, on roads
to nowhere, through the rain, through smoke."
Such was his rhetoric, the while a pair
of maggots wriggled from the corner
of his eye, and curled together in a
glistening ball, their pleasure on his lid.
The little girl tugged his hand, he smiled.

"We should be going. She likes to ride
the escalators." She grinned, pulled him
hurriedly away. And I watched them, linked
by the hand, gliding up and down,
the pair of travelers from 'Ad, then
my announcement sounded. A sudden
fuzz of overlapping zones, and all the baubles
and swankery of golden liquor, shiny
paperbacks, sheer gift-scarves in the tunnel
of bright stores became a formless glitter
—there was a rushing hiss and roar—
but it was only a scheduled takeoff, and I
slid calm and weightless through
the cold, aortal portals of the terminal.

DAUGHTER, PLANETARIUM

She stands enduring, her iPod to her ear
Beside me and the ceiling, whirring, opens.
An ink-wash of Copernicus downstairs;
Up here archaic chain and gears at work.
The teeth are greased, a rotary horizon to pull
The domed night open, but space is huge and
The telescope's data can only be portrayed
In television patterns; yesterday, she stacked
Her chat line messages and multitasked them,
Coped, because as ever the young are skilled
Beyond our mastery and we can never visit
Their futures. The screen pulses the emissions
Of fractal cosmic actors, and my daughter holds
My hand, to drag me yet a ways forward
Towards the serpents argent in the plumes
Of sea storms, at the far quadrants of the known,
Towards the static from the stars.

ANXIETY DREAM 1

Dear Parents of Municipal Underground Worker 5674,

I am writing to express my sincere regret
and profoundest apologies regarding
the unfortunate incident that left
your son among his ancestors too soon
on the morning of the 23rd, and, I suppose
to furnish you with a brief account
of how the tragedy transpired. We met
that morning as arranged beneath the streets
at a juncture of the sewage system
best known for its recent renovation,
a synthetic net along the tunnel walls and roof
designed so your son and others like him
could hang from their wing-claws when on breaks
or while conducting our inspections of the wires
and pipes—our business that morning.
I was surprised to be greeted by not five
workers such as your son but instead
by a number of his comrades exceeding five
and probably in the range of many thousands
calling to each other in piping cries.
I remember blanching at the thought of
all the paperwork. I had no idea in light
of the present economic miracles that your son's
friends were in such need of employment.
I called out a few instructions and on we went,
the workers following me in an impressive cloud
breaking apart in short swoops through the violet
and insufficient light, which changed at the shaft.

In fact it became quite strong, bright, and excited
all your son's company, especially when I began
to climb the ladder toward the street; they formed
a vertical funnel around me and shrieked and
chittered; trying to assist, they hooked
my clothing as I rose and tried to lift me and the air
above me was choked off, the shaft's far hole
was a storm of circling and ever-joining wings
and I could not feel my body, only theirs,
and I lost it, I admit, I panicked, taking no care
I only wanted to break free and that is when
my foot encountered a softer rung and I
pushed down, through your son's delicate
and helpless brain, pieces of which I scraped
from my shoe and sweating, already in a sickening
grief, threw my self upwards in the furry void
to lie gasping with his body in my fist
on the sidewalk where, in a canopy of swiftly
crossing figure eights, as I understand is your custom,
they keened above me as I beat the ground
and tried past reason to reassemble his skull
using my thumb and forefinger, while his friends
summoned the proper authorities. I must
break off. Now, as every afternoon, the sun's
rim blurs and flakes off particles
that only I can see; how rapidly they circle;
how certainly they descend.

Again my condolences,

蝙蝠下凡飞
黑窗万口倍
路上人彷徨
小声步之累

Bian fu xia fan fei
Hei chuang wan kou bei
Lu shang ren pang huang
Xiao sheng bu zhi lei

Bats become mortal fly
Black windows times ten thousand
People wander the streets
Quiet steps so tired.

PRAIRIE LOOKOUT

The boy lags in the last stairwell, his parents
In their awkward Punch and Judy, *There you go,*
Dear, Gracious, Dear, and they blot through
The bright door. The blue is so big
It stuns, wide land raked clean to a limit,
Windbreaks like low green clouds, dust
Rising in a needle-speeding plume.
This panaroma a field trip Father cadged
Like the glove factory, finger-molds dripping
From the rafters like bats. The boy breathes
To a peak, happy, a car is a silverfish glint,
And he feels his place in the obscurities.

He is a long ways from Her Majesty,
Over the horizon in a maze of channels, ports,
And turbaned stevedores, wherefrom she sent
The Centennial train to her subjects, a museum
To traverse the colonies, full of antique maps,
Spade-bearded pioneers, and railway coolies.
We sing *Send Her Victorious* in thanks, he thinks,
And Mother and Father beckon; the clockwork
Bison will inch out in a burry cloud
And pummel up the dirt so he can taste it.

The Centennial train, its leathery Indians.

Her Majesty, and the lanterns wavering in
torch-lit waters.

The table is spread,
waves of gold grain,
gooseberries,
madrigals from the maiden larks.

AN INTRODUCTION TO CHAUCER

We hadde but tramped in the driven snow and pooled
Liberally from our boots whilom Professor Grant appeared
First to us, desiccated minstrel, a walking Jack O'Lantern
On the dole, for his head was lollopingly large
And his bones could have done with a brisk dousing.
He opened his mouth and a rich and tweety reel beganne:
Flemish birds remembering the dawn. We fidgeted,
We shivered, not long off the farm, rudimentary fools.
He told us we were randy fowl about to spawn anew.
The maidens were disgusted, the feeble senile perv.
In the Tabard, nigh the martyr's tomb, he rilled along.
Then one day, he fell ill, and an associate marched in
With a reel-to-reel, his tie snagged in the spool
Of Grant's voice giving lectures from intensive care,
From a tiltabed. He did detail the jolly compagnie
Of his infection inadvertently; the castle-rampart trim
On jerkins worn by miller spirochetes and sickle-headed
Pardoners and prioresses, obnoxious in their reach for mead,
Their single-minded gluttony upon an Ox-au-jus,
Ywending aye the sanguine ways of Grant's anatomy.
We satte in our parkas and imagined all the japes
We'd yet endeavour, the lies ahead, the gradual past
Crescive as an Ottoman moon, an symphonic entropy
Filled us as we filled our scribblers, the winter sun
Yronning down, the tinkle of Grant's voice more tranquil,
Until he stood corporeal afore us, not looking much better.
Though we were wont to quicklie tell him the reverse.
The pallor of a candle, the moistness of a broom,
He gacked his throat two blasts, and he beganne
"…all were this Lande fulfilled with Fairye…"
The sly mink clepeth Alysoun, her eyen merrye

In the back row, though she maketh not a moue,
Yet smirketh at all to her full knowe: Professor Grant
Would topple some day, crumble like wasp-paper
Into smelly motes. Fain would fair Alysoun take notes.

TRACY REGETNIG

Tracy Regetnig sat behind Margaret Brandt,
that was that. Every morning
Margaret turned and leaned on Tracy's desk
and the weekend adventures
flew back and forth with giggles. "Girls!"
went the teacher, and Margaret looked
at the board, till Tracy tapped her—
they were off to their gossip again.

Tracy had a surgical scar
beginning at her collarbone
and ending at her heart, which
stopped that summer.

All August Mr. Regetnig's
18-wheeler sat at the curb
shining in the heat, taller
than their house at the foot
of Worthington Street.

In September, Margaret sat
in the same desk, and her
shoulder would swivel
but she never completed the turn;
she squared her books and paid
attention, like a proper young lady.

GYMNASTICS

At first, I cannot make her out
among the gym-mats, taut wires,
padded bars and heaped-up gym bags
at the meet, the swarm of girlhood
in bright leotards, and then her
lissome figure moves in preparatory
stretches from the gaggle, and, facing
judges, in her heightened zone,
she mounts the beam. She plies
first turns with high-wire wariness,
eyes holding her in plumb,
then plunges to a cartwheel: hand, and hand
come sure and solid on the wood,
but the trailing foot brushes,
misses. She jolts down, and turns on
a smile so artificial it smites me:
she *presents*, as she's been taught,
to audience and judges, hands held out and
high in a Vee, indifferent to fault,
and resumes.

(May she never have to use that skill, no,
never have to ice a catty parry
in the convenience store or arena
parking lot, and stare right through
her rival, smiling. May she never have
to slam the car door, hard, or kick
the curb. Or glide past an ex-husband.
If there's a beam wide enough to hold
her soul, may she wicked stick it.)

When she was hurt, I brought her gel-packs
alternating cold and hot, applied them
to her back, the damage she'd inflicted
by daring to fling gravity
from her will across a springy floor.
Fierce in her ten years, struggling in
enforced stillness, she'd test
her muscles' possibilities in slow-motion
walkovers on the carpet, and in seal-like
arches of her spine; outside, she
vaulted a low bush, automatically
grabbed her back. She said, "It's fine,"
and limped.

She lands the cartwheel, and
boldly skips and plants her hands
and tick-tocks over, one leg bent to
arc her skeleton above her head;
she's quickened in her skill and flies
along the beam in two steps, launches
up, and from a flipping tuck
is suddenly erect and beaming
on the mat (a small corrective step).
So formally does she grin, protract
her pleasure in her outstretched Vee, I see
each callous on her upraised hands.

FRAME

One's family history
plays softly always
in those unlifelike colors
volume down
movie on the far monitor
at the video store

The figures loom
and make their speeches

Shelves of plastic boxes
propose more interesting stories
poses and bosoms
cars, guns and steeds

this summer's audience
their tanned legs
jostle each other into
compromises of entertainment

the sidewalk outside smelling
of tar and bubble gum

while the teenager for whom
movies are still truth
scampers around replacing
returns
                years away
from regret

her eye drifts to the far monitor

where someone with infinite skill
is extracting an apology

VENERATION

After a while, the human mind gets tired,
Grandpa said, and that's why his platoon
was able to gently lift Tommy guns from sleeping
German soldiers in those hot afternoons,
curled up in open basement shells;
they scarcely lifted their eyes when their hands
were lightened; it was no surprise, the smell
of clover overcoming cordite they awoke to
in the Netherlands. A lifetime later, on rare furlough
from the nursing home, Grandpa, no higher
than his wheelchair, pulled up next to
the woman he had once wooed, desired,
his wife of fifty years, and said, Hi, Kay.
Hi, Frank, she said. The human mind gets tired.

MIDWINTER BY THE DRYER-VENT

I am sad to watch my neighbour,
So sad my copula sustains a *Mitteleuropa* weariness,
As he plods behind the bright red snow-blower
To and from the garbage cans
From and to the bungalow;
And I see his grim persistence,
Corvée load of the northern cathedrals,
Is being paid with interest to someone long ago
Who didn't love him—
His hands are cold, his face is cold—
Because he didn't please them—
He is slow because he carves imperative perfection
And he has no balaclava.
Suburban *Mitteleuropa* no balaclava person!
Love is the problem and the question;
For everything else there is credit card and pension.
Love tells us pretty much what to do—
His face protrudes; in the snowbank a concavity—
Until it no longer cares to tell us what to do,
A twilight of scarab-sheen dimension,
The rolling door descends, machine she put away,
And, later, a light in the kitchen.

池旁妙妹竽
何没吹军歌
后悔不礼貌
入水变成鱼

Chi pang miao mei yu
He mei chui jun ger
Hou hui bu li mao
Ru shui bian cheng yu

Pond-side a marvelous Sis and her flute.
Why do you not play the troupe-songs?
Regret is not appropriate, she said
And slipped into her fishness.

POUTINE WITH COMET

Passing snowbanks gleaming on the shoulder
In *the dead of night* just East
Of Brandon, dark tower of the Perogy Palace
Sign my beacon, and beyond the wide spray
Of mercury-vapor light above the Husky,
In a vicious wind, I, I. In a small
Quadrant of the sky, the inching brilliance
Of a comet's spermatozoal tail
A-wriggling for the innocent. I came
From two hours loading pallets, the shrill
Sing-song of metal strapping, heavy-tired,
Impatient, dreaming of pitch black coffee
And a pack and a half of Player's Light.

I had but baffed my hands together
In the doorway of the Husky
When I saw him, Uncle Bobby, hunkered
In the far booth, veteran of aluminum
Feed-trough campaigns here to Edmonton,
Pushing sixty through his tortured bronchia,
Overweight, his Black Cat
Burning in the ashtray. The waitress placed
A plate of hot poutine before him;
Still kicking, he licked his lips and fell to
Sucking cheese-curd out of gloppy gravy,
Lifted a fry and dipped his chin to
Gobble its droop.

He didn't see me. I was stoned, as usual.

If I say Hi now, Hi Uncle Bobby,
There'll be hours of bullshit
Till the truck-lights dim—he was on the road,
He made ends meet, ticker not too bad,
And eventually the whole damn clan would know—
Aunt Flo with her Kleenex balled up
In her cleavage, and her Sunday brunch
Pigs-in-blankets, and Bobby Junior
With his mechanic's-ticket forearms,
And my Granddad with his sling-milk-crates-
For-forty-years-big fingers yelling
(Deaf as dulse) Hello Young Feller—
He would know, and then my Mom
And Dad—I'd been wandering the prairie
In the corpse-glow, my eyes
Like banners for amphetamines,
My beard a startup grow-op, so I ignored
The waitress's cool "Coffee, honey?"

And ran across the parking lot
Behind some trucks and got
On the highway, underneath
That comet and trudged
Till it should overtake me
In its metazoan vector,

Stubborn as I was those days for cinnamon,
A girl named Rackle and her crossover cassettes
Of steel guitars, her kisses, and her sinsemilla skin.

THE KIND

We did the drugs in the late afternoon. When you do drugs,
The go-to drug is The Kind. It's a true-blue drug,
Me and you drug, peace of mind. We did the drugs
At Troy's around a huge spool coffee table.
We did them with Roger Lapointe, an old guy
Who turned sheets with us at the mill. Troy had good drugs,
But not as good as Floyd's, although Floyd's
Had been up and down lately. Roger was into whiskey,
Not drugs, but we liked the example he set.
He called his whiskey Pussing Sipply.
The carpet was shaggy and two-tone, shit and diarrhea.
Floyd showed up with better drugs than usual.
Roger greeted him with, "Love that Pussing Sipply,
Sipply makes it right, Blame the whole damn thing
On Ripley, and do it right, every night." Floyd didn't comment.
We pulverized the buds and loaded the bong,
After a brief argument ultimately rejecting
The raspberry zigzags for the bong. We did the drugs.
After a while Floyd said, "Towards a Canada of Drugs,
That's the ticket. Try to see my vision.
The whole healthcare system, the gleaming tubes
And instruments—the perfect vehicle
For widespread drug delivery." "I phoned my parents."
"You phoned who?" "My parents. I made my case,
Said, but Mom, but Dad, I'm good at drugs. All I ask
Is you stake me. Twenty grand ought to
Kickstart a brilliant career in drugs. Well, better
Make it twenty-five. I also want an Aerosmith
Logo tattooed on my cock." We all laughed. Roger said,
"Sipply, sipply, sipply, do it funky-wa, blame the
Whole damn thing on Ripley, hoo-ha, hoo-ha."

We couldn't respond, really. Floyd reached
For the raspberry zigzags. Troy's iguana was nosing
Around the Hot Wheels cars in his big cage
And his tongue went sissy lisp. "You know what
Don Juan said?" went Troy. "Don Who?" "Don Juan.
He was a *brujo,* heavy wicked sorcery shit. He said,
Only the little smoke will give you the speed
Necessary to catch a glimpse of the fleeting world."
"Oh holy god of drugs," I said, "let me crisp to a cinder
In your glorious fire." Roger was face-down
In the beanbag. "No, hofficer, I nevair smoke
The gan-ja. I come from Rouyn Noranda, she hell
Of a big mine. Hofficer, my car she hit the black hice
And I sailed through the hintersection..." Smoke lay in
A pewter blue layer about our heads. I gave Troy
A twenty for the drugs and stepped outside.
The sun was sinking. I looked back in.
"Happy planet, all on drugs," said Troy,
Filching a pack of smokes from Roger's pocket.
And I was driving around Esquimalt, eyes red,
Primed for the sirens.

CIGARETTE HUMOURS

Fantastic

Where the bee sucks, there suck I,
because it's my own private pack,
peel off the customs strip, and snap
the cellophane away, the brain agog
with "Fresh Deck Weekend" or
"Mondo Filter Summer"; the first drag
has me laser-pointing, ruminant
with the tip, underlining yet again
a parenthetic apology for the thought
of Spinoza, Kant, back in the days
of print discourse and elitist cafés;
a wave, and with my cigarette
I illustrate the wandering
of electrons first explored by a frizzy
haired patent clerk; a smoke-ring, the dross
snorted like a tiny veil into the nostrils.
And my friends all roar, strike matches
with their hands elegantly cupped
and the candelabras blaze in
the Spanish galleon that I've renovated
while connoisseur hot jazz vibrates
the crystal ashtrays and we spin
the packs, trying to get them to land
upwards, after a thrilling afternoon
of parasailing or our part time jobs
as singing picadors.

Whereas I am standing on a balcony
or in the middle of the street,
tapping ash onto my shoes,
the music and laughter tiny,
elsewhere, because everybody's quit.

Commemorative

Twenty-five years ago,
midnight shift, asphalt repair,
the young bucks leaned on
their shovels, packs twisted
in their tee shirt shoulders
and listened to Roger Harris,
the old guy, pushing forty,
hold forth, talking around
his hand and his cigarette
as the ash ate down.
"No job, no education,
and your girlfriend's pregnant,
boys, as the Welsh say,
it's a lovely song."
The asphalt fumes choked
you awake on the deserted
bridge, and every hour
there was a smoke-break.
"I wrote a novel once,"
said Roger, "about a guy
who had an affair with
his stepmother. It was part
autobiographical."
Which part, I wondered,
and then I spoke up,
"Can I have one of those?"
Before long I was buying
them daily, and stowing
packs in my hardhat.

Years later Roger appeared
all gaunt and forced
into a Santa outfit
at the local mall, face sagging,
his fingers the color
of wet shit.

Economic

They creep in at you, smoking
peacefully on the sidewalk,
from all corners of downtown,
in their leather vests and tattoos,
with their duct-taped glasses,
their cowboy boots, their beards,
their junky rashes on their throats,
with their sorry pitches, "Hey, man,
can I BUY one of those off you?"
And you tap one loose, without
negotiation; then begins a fruitless
search through pockets; sometimes
a dime is produced, sometimes not.
You haven't the heart to snatch the smoke back.

You are the nexus of screeching need.

You smoke them down and grind
them out, three to a coffee break;
as you do, they home in, backs
already bent at twenty feet, and
snatch the butts up from around
your feet, until they have a handful.
They ruefully regard the butt with only
sprigs clinging to the filter,
the nothing-butt that's just black ash.
There are mutters; these are tossed.
They crawl off, eyes on the ground.
You glance at your watch, and light another.

Eschatological

The fifth horseman,
addiction,
comes at a clip
through smoking midnight pillars
breaking off chunks
of charcoal and cramming
them in his mouth.

Crows light on his shoulders.

On his chest is carved
a single word:
Tabagisme.

His song to the stars
is a tinny whistle
when he breathes in
and a glassy rasp
when he breathes out.

They pass though a copse
of glistening, bronchial trees that drip
gobbets of green phlegm.

Just a little ways, my love,
he whispers to his steed.

At dawn they are plodding
through an expanse of heavy, wet sand
deeper and deeper

in which the smoker awakens
aware of his diaphragm.

ONE DAY AT A TIME

A beefsteak of a guy with sideburns begins
I'm Anthony. Hello Anthony. We are Anthony too.
I was powerless before my need to watch the Family.
Yeah, and then we placed our hopes in a fucking
Higher power. The osric in the salmon blazer
Is wringing his hands, shaking his pomade.
Tell it like it is, Brother Anthony.
I came to my senses passing Lafarge Concrete
Where we whacked the Bollolini brothers.
What did you do then? What then?
The club for a cool one, watched the goomahs
Play on the pole, I hadda get a gun.
But no. But no, but no, but no--
I made a searching and fearless inventory
Of all my demons and past actions. Like fuck
You were searching!, says a young buck in boots
And shoots him. Anthony lunges, but Anthony grabs him.
Relax, princess, Anthony there's a made guy.
They kiss both cheeks, make their long goodbye.

ANXIETY DREAM 3

Your fiancée is glad to see you,
takes your hand and you traipse
through a public amphitheatre,
where there are several miniature
statues of you commemorating
your exploits in the illicit drug trade,
at which you are suitably modest,
having had no—she laughs
brightly, her hair so black
all colours rage and she takes
you home where you hoped to meet
her mother, but instead face drunken
male relatives in an atmosphere
reminiscent of Nicole Williamson's 1969
Hamlet, a strewn interior of firelight
and scattered loot: they loll on beds soiled
with smeared viands, jewel-crusted goblets,
the farting presence of long-haired,
drooling hounds, the floor unwalkable
due to carcasses of game and outmoded
boiler machinery; the windows give onto bricks,
though the way in had appeared straightforward--
the men sharpen knives and mutter
what you take to be imprecations,
your grammar-book knowledge of their language
proving inadequate to the social task
of objecting to the mighty-chested man,
her father, taking her and kissing her
a long time, and fondling her in his lap
while the men yell vaguely familiar
proverbs concerning animals and paradoxes

which you take to be an encouragement
but before you can comment
on your fiancée's well-advanced intimacy
with her dad the lights go

and the fragrance of cinnamon comes visiting
(and a whimpering off in the darkness,
growing forceful, endearingly familiar).
Someone trips and crashes to the floor,
swears, and a hound's reek sharpens
as it in snuffling increments gets to know
your crotch, and you just know
things are going to settle down,
normalize, you just know it.

湖鼠游泳过
一看再停坐
拉月像缌子
付近来哆嗦

Hu shu you yong guo
Yi kan zai ting zuo
La yue xiang si zi
Fu jin lai duo suo

The lake rat swims past.
We stop and sit.
It pulls the moonlight like a rope
Nearer, and we shiver.

CATHERINE'S EYES

Kindle, as when torch-blown
shadows of seekers
for some remote truth
about the species hushed
at cave-walls and beheld
looming shapes of animals

Crazily at romp in flexure
of their fur, rude in the
pyrite night—shapes
they reverently touched
and, rushing off to tell, scattered
in the world, the visions
flaking off like bird-cries,
wood smoke and raw fields

Where with all good hope
of nothing in particular
she wanders to the edge
of blighted Christendom
and the haggard Knightes return—
their tangled hair and years of beard
awkward Crosse on breastplates
pennants afurl and sunlight
flaming in their mail—

Her crusade of recollection
leads her to a forest pool;
she kneels before the green
reflected canopy; one leaf spins
in its ellipsis
down
       down

Into the Sumerian night.
Incense curls about the faces
of clay figurines, of guesses
at the forces in the stone
corners of a room.
A woman breathing
in the moment before sleep:
her pleasure
in that retinal surrender
of awareness in the darkness
is the world.

COW TV

Evening, and the cottonwood leaves
shimmer, their lightweight seeds
drift slowly through the air and
never land; from the far pasture's tilt

the cows come down, stepping slow
like humans on an escalator
to the pond, hooves sucking
thick mud-rind, muzzles to
cool water. Calves nose between
their mothers' legs for teat.
Mothers look off in the green distance
unimpressed by nearby cars,
mere rubbing surfaces
for sore horns. The largest bull
favours his hind leg—
a barbwire wound.

Young bulls go head to head
the stronger driving back the weaker,
who twists his neck away and
reculer pour mieux sauter
shoves back; dust rises from their scuffle.
A deep low, O a deep low,
is the pond's oval osmosis.

An evening breeze excites the herd
and mass-mounting begins;
brother humping sister humping
father humping niece;
they sportively thrust, then it's over.
They plod back to the pasture,

where they've mislaid tomorrow.

SHREW

We stopped on the path
to watch a shrew, who,
oblivious, began to chew
and fill its belly with grass.
We loved its tiny paws and claws;
it played that grass-stem
like a flute, then startled,
left us peering in
the brush where it went.
Time with you is succulent.

ULTERIOR SHEEP

Stand defiant with their vertically slit eyes
too far apart, their b-movie bedouin faces.

They know about hay and barbwire.
What do you know?

Afternoons, you can hear them
one by one, repeating,

below the farm machinery,
from all corners of the sloping field

"Bah! Who made *you* Ram?
Bah! Who made *you* Ram?"

With their minds, they poke the swarm
into the apiary, out, like a loose black napkin.

They turn their bums to you,
spill glistening shit.

At night, at a signal
all know implicitly
they circle the hot tub's
gazebo enclosure

absorbing the jet-sounds,
the tinkle of glasses,
the laughter, the splashes,

and then at a signal
all know implicitly
disperse to dot fields
sloping up from the ocean.

The seven-pointed Dipper
twinkles to scour their
ruby aortas.

They stand at enigmatic
angles to each other
scoffing at walked dogs.

Hay. And barbwire.
The humans helplessly carry coffees.
Their ankles are useless.
A mistake, soon.

SLUGS, MATING

The full moon is a distant palace,
didn't you know, gone.

The slugs trace slime,
antennas like the horns

of patriarchal sacrifices, slither
down the porch column

to twine, snake-like,
until their tongues creep out,

probe, and enter the meniscal
tension between is and are,

Ishtar. The tongue-knot
swells into a tesseractal,

starlit dancehall
where your more casual alleles in tuxedos

and slinky numbers lean
into martinis to the tinkling

stylings of a similarly horny orchestra,
and their eyes met across a crowded room,

but after a few minutes'
mix, tongues come undone,

and slugs are once again dark
lozenges on column,
then the column only,

and the moon a distant palace
for the morning star,

didn't you know?

OWL AND THE UNBORN

Spring trail of mud and slugs.
You halt and whisper *owl:*
it blasts from the loamy floor
of needles, cones and vole-holes,
strobing through the branches,
to land in a recessed apse,
nothing too small to pierce its brain.
We lapse into a worship;

it cowls its wings, folds them back,
shuffles its claws and looks at us,
imperious fledged egg, as a lazy
amniotic sunlight sparkles the bark
in dappling plasma. We hush
and take small steps, drawn to the orb
of its face, the cat-ears and the oval
inset eyes, strange as the gaze

of the girl we lost, in a spasm,
in a gush, the bloody allantois
wet and sticky on your legs.
Her voice the music soothing
through toy-cluttered rooms, handprints
on every surface, and the chance
to miss what I had never wished—
your careworn future loveliness—

passes, and the owl bursts
and glides to another branch.

Spring trail of mud and slugs.

A POEM FOR RAMADAN

After cups of cardamom-laced coffee,
and medjool dates, we said farewell,
for the festival had bled into the evening.
Amal, and her friend Amal,
led me down the spiral staircase.
Amal said suddenly, "My aunt lost
her child in a distant city. *Wallah,*
I cannot imagine a greater pain, to never know
what became of him, not ten years old."
Her friend Amal's eyes teared unbidden;
she whispered, *"Wa waladin wa ma walada,"*
(By the mystic ties between parent and child);
Amal nodded and rejoined,
"Laqad khalaqna al-insan fi kabadin,"
(Verily we created man into a condition).
Which was pain, we knew together,
spreading in that woman's search—
cities and faces and interminable streets
in a hell of a big world. Amal and Amal
held hands, ribosomes in plain white robes
on a spiral staircase, bearing sorrow's code,
and two names meaning hope.

你和我找到小石
在海滩拿起来它
后来方地上走了
现在手指都有沙

Ni he wo zhao dao xiao shi
Zai hai tan na qi lai ta
Hou lai fang di shang zou le
Xian zai shou zhi dou you sha

You and I found a small stone
On the beach and picked it up
Then put it down and walked on
—Now our fingers are sandy.

LIVING WITH THE LAMA

Twenty minutes in, when the Buddha is glowing in you.
Through to the root of my anxiety.
Through the fontanel.

The most adept of monks.
Tapped the glass—he saw into me.
Slipped my daughter a marzipan pig.

She quickly acquired a taste for marzipan.
There was glass between us.
Ran into him chowing down at KFC.

Practice *powa,* letting go of the soul.
No one in the temple missed his water-pistol awakenings.
May this help me to ease the pain of separation.

Like unto us and enlightenment.
Kadampa monks repeat when faced with disaster.
I had the apartment number but not the entrance code.

I choked I never did nirvana very well.
We were on the same realm after all.
He reached under his cushion, and produced the pig.

With one bite, my daughter attained enlightenment.

BODHISATTVA

I go to such a Zen place with Tim,
former All-World centre for San Antonio.
He sets his basketball trophies on the lawn
in his bare feet, grinning,
and topples them with the hose—
the golden posing athletes—
and hummingbirds from up the canyon
dart among droplets with Tim.
He laughs and laughs.
I say, "You wait so long in the post
before you launch your bank shot."
"I didn't shoot the ball," Tim says,
"it just looked that way."
He holds court with his charity people,
a latter-day United Nations.
Tim prefers the quarterly reports,
but he is laid-back about it.
With his dreamy eyes and wide jaw,
Tim would have made a good Amish.
He laughs, and laughs, and laughs.

We go for our evening stroll. "The 40-foot
replay images of us on scoreboards,"
Tim says quietly. "The posters, the close-ups,
the profiles, the slow-mo isolation.
I knew we were being translated
to another realm, but where?"
We listen to the crystal-crashing breakers.
He laughs. Tim laughs and laughs.

The sea, the sky, the rocks, all the same mauve.
Breakers darkening the sands of Topanga.
"I no longer fear it," Tim says.
We are still until invisible.

BASKETBALL ANECDOTES

They meet in the bar with their plasticized
clipboards with courts drawn on them
and little magnet-pucks symbolizing players.
They seek only formless story, storyless form:

"Martin Riley saved up the money himself
working at his uncle's vacuum shop
to go to the National Team tryouts in 1973.
He brought his own basketball, first day
of tryouts he walked into the gym
totally cut, bursting out of the red and white
pinney they gave him, and calmly
unzipped his gym bag, producing his Wilson Jet.
It had so many floor hours,
dark at the seams and slippery.
He used it in all the individual drills.
Where did Martin come from? He came
from lonely prairie gyms, where
there was no sound but the bouncing ball.
Five-eleven, leg spring zero,
but a basketball machine, such solid fundamentals
he got out and ran his squad
in scrimmages, the other guards never once
killed his dribble, Martin,
zipping perfect passes to the big men from
a commanding top of the key.

"Come the Olympics the American
Quinn Buckner shut Martin down.
Buckner, who lettered too in football,
and had survived Bobby Knight's
tyranny at Indiana. Against Quinn's swarming arms
and treetrunk legs, Martin dribbled standstill;
Quinn made him travel miles
out of his way to bring the ball up court;
the once perfect passes sailed
into the stands; Quinn cut
him off and Martin pivoted madly,
looking for the open man from a good
thirty feet. At the other end, Quinn
stutter-stepped and blew past Martin
into the paint, like a man casually opening
a door and inviting himself in,
drawing defense so he dished out dressily
for easy lay-ups. Just goes to show."

"Bobby Knight. He ran a coaching clinic
up here, gave a little talk on motivation.
Asked for a volunteer and said,
'Would you please run down the court
and back?' which someone did,
at a reasonable pace.
Then Knight went rat-shit, grabbed the kid
and screamed, 'Do it again, you candy-ass
excuse for a worthless shit-licking
hound-dog id-jit,' and took a chair
and whipped it at him (it bounced real high).
The kid did somewhat improve his time.
Knight turned to the other coaches,
spread his hands, 'That's motivation.'"

"Art Tatum rose
like an onyx sword from
downtown, the crowd's breath
on the backs of his knees, the ball
released far above his head
by his pink-pad fingertips,
a smooth and regular
rotation that met
nothing but net."

"Clyde van Cayzell showed up at summer camp
with his crossed eyes, his herky-jerky
waist-high dribble. He came off picks
and launched, like drawing a bow and firing,
angular. He came to camp for one reason
and one reason only—to beat Martin Riley.
He went one on one with him every day,
the results being somewhat comic.
Martin wiggled his chin and Clyde would *sky*—
jockstrap in the rafters—and down
he came, and Martin cocked his eyebrow—up
Clyde leapt again—until Clyde knew, just
knew Martin would fake, stayed rooted
—Martin casually banked the ball in.
Martin beat him forty-two straight times, until
Clyde, up 10-9, game to 11, took Martin baseline,
and finished with a finger-roll that hit one rim,
the other, and plopped in. Martin grabbed
the ball immediately —'Another?', but Clyde
squeezed his crossed eyes shut, *'No.'*
He wanted to savour the win."

"Against Northwest Minot Junior
Technical State they came out from the tip
and drained their first eighteen from outside.
They played like we weren't there.
I looked at the clock: we were down
thirty-eight to two after seven minutes.
'Put a hand in their face, gol-dang it!'
yelled the coach, and we tried, we even pressed,
and their point guard ran a dribbling clinic.
We finally got a basket, and handed the ball
out of bounds to their power forward, who said,
'Preciate your effort, white.'

"After the Minot game, we were having coffee
in the motel lounge with the coach
underneath this huge stuffed pickerel
on a plaque, and who should walk
in from the parking lot but the
towering hulk of *Howard Lockhart,*
in a great coat. Lockhart was scouting
for the NBA, those days. The coach
knew him from way back; he sat with us,
and we all noticed the jewel-studded
NCAA rings on his massive hands.
'Howard here played with *John Havlicek*
at Ohio State,' the coach said.

"Now, Howard Lockhart
sipped from the tiny cup and regarded us
suspiciously, as meat slung in an open stall.
We braved the raw force of his handshakes.
Then Abby, who was from Harlem, stood
and said, 'That fish shouldn't be talking
that shit, you hear it?' Three silences ensued:
the silence of nothing having happened;
the silence of it was Abby's business if indeed
something had happened (he'd obviously taken
some awesome drug to get him through
the road trip); and the final silence
of mettle-awareness, Howard being the judge.
He brushed crumbs off the table, and said,
'You boys better per-form for Jerry, hear?'
and then he was crossing the parking lot,
Styrofoam cup in hand, to his El Camino,

well into his last years as a scout, Lockhart
driving from gym to gym across the heartland,
with an ever-present coffee in his fist, crouched
in the stands, waiting, eyes hooded, waiting
for the flashy guard to throw the ball away
on the fast break, waiting for the iffy forward
to turn the corner with his weak hand,
tomahawk it down, the backboard
shattering glass like hail, but mostly waiting
for the faint hiss of the showers, the young fans
dragging coats behind them as they leave,
the ball that rolls into the corner, the referee
who packs up his gym bag in the stands."

ON FIRST LOOKING INTO ALLEN IVERSON

I used to drive by the junkyards and the gold
River in my superturbo *Answering Machine*,
And turn the heat way up, coz it was cold,
Watching the factory smoke rise still and clean,
And I never had no doubt I'd get old,
One in a million, superstar, and cruising
Past the Projects, remembered I'd been told
I'd end up dribbling circles round them, and losing
Anyway. But I got the bling. I looked in my mirror
And I will never forget—saw this skinny wigger
Wearing my line of kicks, yo, I got out
Signed his kicks and told him, memories, bury them
Anywhere you can. Your rearview getting clearer.
Coz time runs out. Coz there ain't no doubt.
Coz his name was Darien.

THE BLOSSOMS OF CHANG'AN

After years in government, a belly
and buttons that pull apart. One glimpses
leaving the washroom one's tonsure.

Ripping up and planking down
the same language—policy options
and downstream costs—has worn

a hole in time, through which one
sees liver-spotted hands
riffling through papyri.

The silk suits and blazing ties
cruise through the grey halls
and palm the latest quick-talk toys.

Younger Colleague seems more
and more to preface his remarks
with "My generation,"

as he selects a shirt and tie
from his cubicle wardrobe,
having settled in for the long haul,

"My generation wonders what to do
with so many boomers still around—
I wonder if I really want

to be a deputy minister,
pressure from above and below.
The policy wheel keeps turning."

At lunch the females troop out
to shop, returning to the building
with what is rightfully theirs,

bright bags of purchases.
There are numerous passwords
required to do the public's business—

the public! A stalking beast,
its righteous scrutiny a legend,
its deep fear of change a legend.

At times one forgets
what is in fashion—
centralized or regionalized.

One supports decisions
which will never get made;
at coffee, the talk is of sensible

plans for mortgages and vacations.
Younger colleague confides in you:
"Retirement, what I don't get

is I won't be here,
and all these important public
policy issues will continue."

The land is alternately governed
by entrepreneurial zealots
and socialist fantasists.

The city spreads out from
one's window into folding,
purple, distant hills.

And in the late afternoons,
deep in the monitor, behind the glyphs,
in springtime where once rode

the successful young scholar,
slowly, softly, ceaselessly fall
the blossoms of Chang'an.

想看一只狼
疑是雪皮梦
鼻到尾快闪
真假都一样
反而贴在桑
原来本身声
如此人无家
盲流无祖宗

Xiang kan yi zhi lang
Yi shi xue pi meng
Bi dao wei kuai shan
Zhen jia dou yi yang
Fan er tie zai sang
Yuan lai ben shen sheng
Ru ci ren wu jia
Mang liu wu zu zong

Thought I saw a wolf
Perhaps a snow-skin dream
Nose-tail flashed real-false
Capable of in-between
But it stuck in my throat
My voice's predecessor
A floating labourer
With neither home nor ancestor

THE ROAD TO PONTEILLA

In spring I took to *la ronde*
left for Ponteilla
warehouses and loading docks
a slim stick in watery distance
slowly grew blacker—
an Asian man my age
smirched with grease and dust
suppose he'd gotten off work
crawling away from
some hourly abuse to go lie
in a stupor but mostly
I thought about myself—

We passed each other with a civil nod
under a billboard with a buxom *belle*
yanking a *mec* towards her lusciousness
by his tie—*Plaisir et seduire*—
Les Vins de Roussillon!

I wasn't him in passing
—complacency or *complaisance?*
—but couldn't pause, eager to spend
the mint coin of the realm;
soon enough the breeze in silver poplars
shivering and shuttering
distracted me near Ponteilla,
though I had sincerely meant
to find myself:

Faux-dauphin du macadam.

MEANWHILE EVIDENCE OF ADMIRAL ZHENG HE'S 1421-23 EXPEDITION TO NORTH AMERICA CONTINUES TO ACCUMULATE

A researcher learns that Alabama has four-word proverbs, just like in China. He drives all night to interview the oldest living expert. He has an exuberant Adam's apple and sits in a rocking chair on the porch chewing tobacco.

Understand you got four word proverbs here in Bama.
Most do, even those that think they ain't.
Are there very many of them?
Yep.

What are they about?
Most got to do with them badass Grackle boys.
I could give you a sample: "Guard Dies Grackle Swings."
What does it mean?
It means it was surefire gonna happen, one way or other.
Or "Rabbit Test Pins Grackle": what goes around comes around.
Are any of them not about the Grackles?
Well there's "Gator Gator, Later Later". Means you got the hell out.
And are any of them more than four words long?
I was gonna mention "Grackles Gone Bobby-Sue's Prom",
But some of us experts done count Bobby-Sue as one word.

CANZONE FOR FOREIGN EXPERTS

"Meeting in Beijing, Sailing in Qingdao," is all I've heard
This year in Qingdao, China. "One World, One Dream"
Is another slogan *en passant dans l'air.* I've also heard
China has banned plastic bags; a crinkly flock is heard
Snapping past, snagging on branches, in full flight
From their prohibition. When you've heard
One plastic bag, or a jellyfish tornado of them, you've heard
Them all. The slogans are spoken by men
With plastic faces, peel-off masks, stick-on, Party men
Velcroed to their platforms. We've all heard
Such bilge before, unenforceable laws, artificial joy
And the sun sets *couchant* in a coaly red, inspiring joy.

The pessimistic negative becomes a sort of joy.
The rattle in all the children's laughter that you've heard.
In my senior class there are twelve girls named Joy:
Mopsy Joy, Schoolmarm Joy, Model Joy and Bright Joy
Among others. At roll call, Joy's no absent dream.
Dare I ask them to taste a grape with Joy's
Strenuous tongue? I think not. Dean Wang's a kill-joy
And he's watching me. In paranoid flights
My foreign tendencies emerge, the round-eye flight
From reformer to conformist; in plagiarism I find joy
And chalk-dust. The nearly women, nearly men
Listen politely, the women quietly modest, the men

Bristling with adverse identity, proud, because as men
They must defend against direct outlandish joy
That skewers substitute teachers elsewhere, the timid men
Who blanch at spitballs and passed notes; only men
Here can be class-monitors, or so I've heard.
"Are we mere test-takers, or living women, living men?"
I rant. Several fall asleep at this. "If men
Made universities for China's progress," I insist, "that dream
Appears to be failing us!" Is this a dream
Or did someone respond? One of the men?
The class is panicked now, wanting to take flight.
Only 30 more hours in class, and I get a return flight

To Canada, free of charge, an economy-class flight
Rubbing shoulders with the jetblack, dye-job Party men
And their smug *tai-tais,* a twelve hour flight
No smoking all the way; on screen Hong Kong mobsters flyte
Against each other. Crowdedness doesn't faze me; it's a joy
To be less than an individual, and take flight
From my inbred selfishness. "During the flight
Please keep seatbelts fastened, seatbacks upright," is heard
Amid the tonal slalom babble of Mandarin, heard
Now from Vancouver to Ulan Bator, Hans in flight
From the gap between rich and poor, and as I dream
Of cheeseburgers, they of Richmond's condos, same dream,

Different meanings. In the village eating meat's a dream
And so is dentistry, inoculation, Chang-E's unlikely flight
And central heating, even a decent parka: TV dreams
That even a dog must have: snout-twitching dream
Of being unbraised, unfried, not chopsticked by men
Who sleep the winter away in a communal dream
Of filial sons whose Party ranks are a dream
Dilution of despair, a forward-filing joy
To all descendants. But, bored by merely seasonal joy
And suffering, they stir themselves from dreams
Of luxury and ease, and come awake, "You've heard
The *yuan* is rising; China will rise again!" is heard.

But "Meeting in Beijing, Sailing in Qingdao" is what I've heard
Over and over, a looping, pleasing corporate dream.
In satellite darkness we pause in our flight
From reality to fiscal fantasy, last century's men
And women, to taste the tin diaspora of joy.

QINGDAO'S "ANGRY YOUTH" FLIRT WITH A ROCOCO "INTERNATIONAL" STYLE WHILE HOLDING OUT FOR SUPREMACY

Tan smoothness inked with dental instruments produces a *petit-point* village—pigs, ducks, minor officials. Under the lid, a sawn and glued smell. Say to the foreigner: I do not know if it is genuine leather. I do not know.

Bamboo screens, small lantern-light on leaves, and bamboo stands indicate concealment of the more elitist *chaguars,* wherein wait pressed millstones of dark tea, and aged *pu-er,* kept in caves to cultivate an invigorating mould.

Wood stools so small they literally, squatted on, cannot be seen.

Banners and lanterns above, crinkly chilis in oil below—red Earth the mirror of Heaven—and tall girls in red silk *qipaos* peregrinating in between: the hungry ghosts.

Alternately listen for the song of zero and the song of sparrow.

The Party class-monitor stood and said she believed one ought to dress according to one's station. Maybe so, but the hair-bun, earlobes, clavicle, wrist-bones, waist-band, panels, seams and flares should not be unadorned.

The soft suitcase you lug, or drag, must have at minimum plaid or cartoon animal.

Whatever are the student troops-in-training *thinking* with their blue camo? A barrage of harmless bubbles?

Plaster becomes particular like coal-spend pilfering the cilia. Smear the passenger seat-belts with axle-grease and you need never feel inferior.

A pan of fried scorpions resembles rusty jumbled screws and hooks. Sidewalk hatchbacks jaw open. Transparent teeth—vials of perfume.

SUBJUNCTIVE MOOD ON HAINAN ISLAND

That delirious day of Spring Festival,
We skipped from a mirrored boutique
Into a street of wobbling tangerine loads
And glorious litter—red crêpe strips
Of black grass-style calligraphy
Dusted with firecracker-ash.
I nearly tripped over a box.

Inside was a beggar, folded, bent
Backwards, pinned by thick lacing—
Were those strips of skin?
The corners of his eyes pulled
Back, too. We stumbled
On, into a wide ring of shoppers
Arms crossed, bored, dangling bags.

The orangutans were chained in a
Ragged gang at the ankles,
Just as the folktale predicted:
Drunk monkeys, drunk monkeys,
Slipping on, lacing up interlinked sandals,
proving their prison. Tricked!
With a pensive, simian patience,
They hopped on their cardboard boxes.

Their casual master raised a fistful of *kuai*
To the crowd, then a coir whip.
The legs of passers-by would persist,
Festival after festival, and never provide
A clear path for that beggar to lock eyes
With the monkeys, across the dust,
Not for one instant.

O LITTLE TOWN OF HANKOU

Coal-poisoned snow is falling on the little town
Of Hankou and the No. 3 Steel Mill, whose stacks
And parapets fold smoke into the gelid cold.
Worker No. 1311, a Wang Jian Guo, fishing
Sooty flash beneath a conveyor, runs out of luck,
The struts above him, having met their bending
Moment, give; the tonnage plunges, crushing legs, torso
And lungs, to pin him face-up in the roar
Of wheeling galactic catwalks, a pulp of pain, but change
Is general in the world of the ten thousand things:

An accidental angle allows Wang, through a crack
Between Numbers 5 and 7 hoppers, and an open door,
Visual access to the foreman's office and the generously
Sized TV. Flanges clank, turbines whine, steam blasts,
But on TV—he fights to breathe—a beautiful boy
Rises slowly on a platform among laser-sweeps and
Artificial storms of petals as his budding lips
Sing now of love in public squares, on golden beaches,
Love forever like loyal swallows, a promise over noodles,
As he strolls among flung roses, singing of love,

The centre of the world for those who hear him sing.
The many-headed crowd waves blinking signs and sways;
The social corpus, ranked in work units, enthuses—nurses,
Brave sailors, construction grunts in safety helmets, dignitaries
With smooth, bland faces, waving their complimentary logos:
One Love, One Planet; the boy-star is mobbed by
Selected children. Wang cannot breathe. Voices, boots:
"We need to be unanimous on this." "The slowdown,
The airlift. Not to mention. Rehabilitation. The numbers
Speak for themselves." "Hao." "Hao." "*Bu* hao."

"We're losing money as we speak." "*Twenty years!*"
"You want to tell them, then? That's settled. Close down
This area; by swing shift it will be over." "*Bu hao.*"
"*I said unanimous.*" "Xing." "Xing." Boots walk away.
The clanking becomes furious. On TV the beautiful boy
Is beckoning to someone, then his eyes raise, and fill
With glee as rainbow bubbles wander in his vision.
Wang shudders, looks down on Hankou in the snow,
Dark million footprints merging, the character for Spring
Will soon be hung on every door, and soon inverted.

In a related story, Shandong Province marine biologists
recently found in the deep silt of the Zhong Hua es-
tuary a one-point-eight-meter fish with stunted arms
and legs. Party spokesmen called the find "significant"
and "the next evolutionary stage." It was crawling away
from humanity.

THE SHANDONG DEAD

The shack crammed with greased car-parts, weighed
Down by roof tiles, sinks deeper into yellow dust.

Inside, a case of *pijiu* is diminishing gout by glug
In rude dispute, in lusty roars. Fingers get thrust

In eye sockets, shins are kicked, mouths twist hard
To swizzle and puke. Wang gets up, brains himself,

Crumples like a slit pig. Li pours 80 proof
baijiu on his hair until he curses, farts and cracks

another bottle. "You owe me one," says Wang.
"I'll take your wife," Li goes, "as she's pinning

Your crusties to the line, come up behind her,
Squirt, hey, another Li, set up for the dust."

Raises his glass. "To the dust." "She's too *pu-su*
For you. She likes her sausage from her cabbie

And her cadre, what am I, a fool? Here's Zhou."
Zhou comes through the wall, all glistening black.

"Ho-ho what have we here, the funky monkey?"
"I sleep in heaps of coal, for kicks," Zhou snorts

Out an anthracite mist. "Totally refreshing,
How's tricks?" "Same old, got a welder last night

Overtime, the condo site. Cut his line, flicked his
Bic, fried him like a stick of haws. Scaffold's still

Knocking against concrete. He'll be by. I like
To get 'em when they've totally forgot—"

"What they did to you! What they did to you!", three
Chant together, grin like boys with scabby knees.

"Mine is the foxy hotties, best during military training
Or before a test, some fun, they shiver and sweat,

Lick them where I like to, that's the best."
The bottles clink, they drink. "This one's off."

"That so?" "Yeah, tastes like—Zhou, you filthy
Egg." "Thought I'd give you a refill, Little Wang."

"Li, what recent measures for your pleasure?"
"Goalies, I trip them during penalty kicks."

They pause, and listen to the city's throb and tick.
They belch, and listen to the swarming sickness

Known as life. "The idiots, what do they think?
They're all gonna get rich? Be glorious?"

"Thinking, tell you, that's one thing I don't miss.
Look here, who's this?" And Chen slips through

The rafters, a mite frizzled about the skin.
"Chen! *Hao jiu bu jian!*" "Okay, which one

Of you idiots made me hover like a deep-fried bat
All day at my miserable funeral, yum-yum,

I can already taste those maggoty dumplings
on my grave, what, we're still drinking

This shitty *jiu*, some things don't change.
Shove over. Well now you're stuck with me.

Where are the women?" "You don't know?"
"Tell him, Li." "They go to a spa and soak

Their dried-up quims in tubs of vinegar
And little minnows swim up to their nipples,

Simpering you're beautiful, so beautiful, I'll
Nibble you till endless sky and boundless oceans,

What they deserve. Here's money tucked
Into your ribcage." "And where's old Ma?"

"Ma, he's crazy." "Lost it." "Crackers. He went
And attached himself to one of those vanes

On a wind harvester, in the next county, and revolves,
Round and round, blissful as a cretin, dawn

To crows-come, humming Deng Li Jun songs,
what a freak. It was what he wanted to do

with his death."

破房排就拆
没食味腐败
窗门愿波铁
死骨愿米柴

Po fang pai jiu chai
Mei shi wei fu bai
Chuang men yuan bo tie
Si gu yuan mi chai

Wrecked houses in a row
No smell of rot or food
Windows doors want glass and steel
Dead bones want rice and fuel

CAREER PATH

Tries to "dead" his duckie-book in bathtub.
Has vision of courtly life surrounded by
Twelve-year-old girls named Eileen.

Affects hobo dress and manners in teens.
Reads Classics Comics *#73—Siddhartha.*
Declares shoplifting the ultimate poem.

First book: *The Milkmaid's Revenge*
Sells thirteen copies, and is called promising.
Snubs future critic. Snubs litmag editor.

Says, "The road is my never-ending text."
In first flush of Third-Worldism, composes poems
In the voices of Khayyam, Confucius, Diocletian.

Attempts poem about girlfriend's grandmother
Who lived near a mushroom farm. It stinks.
Watches "O Lucky Man" four times in a weekend.

Friendship with Wystan Albert-Ross,
The dry-cleaning poet. Rhymes duck
With fuck. Drinks rye without blanching.

In first flush of Post-colonialism, composes poems
In the voices of Kipling, Arnold Bennett, Pound.
Says, "Only in form do I find my freedom."

Moves to Turnriver, Saskatchewan. Annoys
Farmers at the Husky with his stupid questions.
Declares "Nuns Fret Not At Convent Door"

The greatest sonnet in the English language.
Moves back to West Coast. In first flush
Of Anti-globalism, composes poems

In the voices of the Haida Gwaii poets, whom he calls
"Those perennial and necessary masters."
Second book, *In For a Penny,* sells thirty copies.

Is forced to choose between the prairie hedgehogs
Who know only one thing, the bigness of the sky,
And Montreal foxes, who know mondo.

Can't make up his mind. Composes poem
In the voice of drifting cosmonaut. Snubbed
By Montreal and Prairie prize juries.

Wystan Albert-Ross publishes *Naughtiness,*
A tell-all memoir portraying him
As a paranoid dipsomaniac with urgings.

Absorbs himself in the local. Acquires
Reclusive reputation. In first flush
Of New Tribalism composes poems

In voices of Milošević, Amin, Oppenheimer.
Is called a misogynist in print. Defends himself:
"My necessary *Milkmaid* honoured Woman

And her Soul, way back when."
Writes own blurbs for third book, *Esemplasy,*
Which sells forty-three copies. Charged

With shoplifting. Found dead with duckie.

IMAN

Is it, fundamentally, memory of an ancient
Event, angel towering to the firmament,
(Yet two bow-lengths away), the buzz
In Muhammad's tympani, becoming roar, becoming
First words of an elevated discourse
That astonished the first converts with *iman*.
Or flickering conscience now lacquering, now
Flaking off the mental furniture, each
Deviate layer recorded? Would it resemble,
Swelling and subsiding, some medical display
Or economic model, sine above abscissa,
That beckons and reckons as we rot?
A yen for the rhetorical as you watch
Your fellow bipeds pad their shoulders
To look imposing, strain to tactically
Agree *and* disagree, squeeze another rung
Out of their talky-boxes, position themselves
Among choirs of squeaky chalk,
Stelae of broken chalk. Contrary hum
To tune to, *It makes no difference*
If you declare it openly or keep it hidden,
Though who can reliably dial the station?
Lately there's been much use of the verb
'To channel' in literary criticism, but twilight
Skies arrive from nowhere, rendering breath
Milles-feuilles, fuchsia, lemon, apricot,
Meringue—palette with no answer—
And there is no flaw in it, none; however,

The days are micro-layers of cat-hair,
Resentments, debts, slivers of aromatic
Cheese beneath the fingernails, and
Cream somersaulting in the dregs,
Something to believe in, easily
Enough for all the world mistaken.

INCARNATION

1

I pulled the boxed-up monitors
over slightly warm asphalt
on my bike. I was named for
an outlying district, and my eyes met
his, rising from a manhole, sales banners
across intersections, another set of eyes
two-stepping stairs, one of
the many autumns I have left. The air
smelled like sweet potato skin. I steadily
lugged along, they crissed, they chatted:
all could be shown on the monitors, were
it possible that all be shown. Dropped them,
slurped noodles, loaded up
with hard-drives, component
of the dimming streets, no less
than you who passed me
in fluorescent sweats.

2

I lived on an island. My friend
showed up while I was washing a pig.
I stopped washing the pig. She had had
such big eyes for a long while,
and slipped a string of shells on my wrist.
My father saw us together,
released us to the afternoon.
On the shade-banded island heat blares
from each gesture, so we walked slowly in the sand,
stilling ourselves, slow girl, your family
sold you into the city, called me sister.
The bats flew out over the sea at twilight.
Walked home alone, past squatting boys,
their hands wet with fish,
precarious.

3

I swallowed porridge.
I saw the rail lines run away
and heard of their return,
-smelling of cold mud and vistas.
I dreamed Tsvetaeva stirring cabbage.
Tell me what can hurt,
and I will tell you what hurts.
I sipped for instance frappuccino,
and just stretched out my legs and queen of seeing
piled to the heavens goods, the goods and fools
to rifle them, the floors of silk,
the leather and the little-wheeled conveniences,
and the simple thrill of jewellery, oh, I see
my lifestyle in a magazine,
a moped, a *da ge da*, a gel-job,
a call in the middle of the night.
And the goods piled to high heaven in my eyes.

I know. I know. I know.

EMPTY TEMPLE

Luan qi ba zao, the throngs are slipping away,
the slit robes showing legs, *luan qi ba zao,*
half of them you never talked to, *luan qi*
ba zao, the stones are cold and tightly-fitted,
luan qi ba zao, the calligraphy hangs high
and mighty, *wei shi shi biao,* the candles gutter
in invasive breezes, *luan qi ba zao,*
the temple's empty.

No way of telling if
fern ascending is
as real as fern descending
in the pond. Insects and steam
confuse the issue. Persimmons
rot. Gold koi turn
a murky circle.

You will tell the first person you see
about this empty temple.
You wipe your brow.

Be named at the new moon.
Don't overchew your food.

Luan qi ba zao: At sevens and eights; utter confusion
Wei shi shi biao. Confucian maxim: "Be a teacher to the world."

咱秋天爬山
快跑得太懒
黄叶上下烧
漂流太阳电

Zan qiu tian pa shan
Kuai pao de tai lan
Huang ye shang xia shao
Piao liu tai yang dian

Fall, we climb the mountain,
Too lazy to run.
Yellow leaves burn above, below,
We float in the sun's power.

THE HUMANS

How I had hoped to achieve!
I dedicate this bronze with carved animals
to the glory of my ancestors, forever.

There was scope for knowledge:
everything expands, then bends
back, bends back until light
behaves like black.

Here my prosody: *the terrorists*
in swiftest coruscation
incensed two erections.

And the changing weather:
the hu-qin, 'oud and dulcimer all enjoyed
mild favour with regionally flavoured
ensembles; all have been superseded
by the rain-stick, didgeridoo and panflutes
in sheer number of recordings.

What I meant to say—

AQUINO

The plane begins its descent and
we see the exiled leader calmly
folding and refolding his newspaper,
adjusting his glasses, peer over them
at the too attendant stewardess
with her drink tray, nod briefly to
an advisor over his shoulder.

The green turtles of the Philippines
rise in the Pacific.

Already he can smell the noodle shops,
pineapples and coconuts piled in stalls,
brown-legged millions pressed against
the sea, the silk-shirted bands in air-con
bars, dark-haired girls in flip-flops,
American bucks peeled off in backstreets
and wider yet, in the misty hills
the life-size crucifixes borne by the devoted—
all to whom his name means something
valuable, elusive, difficult to form
out of the multitude, though the inky
Tagalog newspapers even now
proclaim it, his arrival, so-called
hope of the people.

The writerly quest for convincing detail
erasing what the subject knows;
there is no way to enter him completely.
In such men there builds
an imminence, a fatal certainty.

They are the event that masses, brooding
cumulosity, over the heads of others.
They rise to quote themselves, crackling
in the flash-bulb brightness, aware
of the endless moneyed conduits opening
beneath them, of the sweet, distinct
plummet into history.

He knew full well.

The stewardess kindly informs him
to fasten his seatbelt. Around him
briefcases get snapped shut and stowed
beneath the seat in front. An intercom
voice says something about final approach.
This before laptops, before cell phones,
palm-pilots, still a taped world.
Hours ago he gave an interview,
was avuncular, expansive, waved
his glasses to make a point, the camera
whirring...

He rolls down his sleeves, bends
to scratch the bottoms of his feet,
slips on his shoes. He reads again
a story from the *Times,* or appears to.
A hand on his shoulder; he waves it off.
He knows full well. He stretches
and watches the ground rushing up,
the lights at the end of the runway,
the wheels bouncing, once, twice.
He ties his shoes.

In modern memory his name ranked
against the legends of scores of closets
of Italian, leather, multicoloured shoes.

They will remember Imelda's shoes.

The reporters bump and press against
each other on the tarmac, huge sweat-
stains on their white shirts, aware of
the 48 point bold face type ahead:
if it were to happen, would they still
have time to file their stories? They
look around at the assembled groups,
nervous. Cigarettes are hurled down,
crushed under heels. The stepladder
is wheeled up to the plane. Naïveté,
the stories are already written, lead
and B-copy, will be released
at a single affirmative word.

Aquino steps off the plane,
carpet, tarmac, the smell of fuel,
the brace of voices, and a single figure
blurring, the ringing shots—

THE LIBRARY AT ALEXANDRIA

In all likelihood draughty, oil lamps
On low flutter, more than one potion
Would have had to be muttered here,
Among the racks of plant-matter, stinking,
Cocoonish—yet the polished bodies
Of attendants (Do you think a library
Is unipurpose?) would have led you,
As a blinkered Arabian is led,
By your lips, your inconceivable tongue,
Into the antechamber of questions
Past all confronting, would confront you past
Your curiosity into a plenteous map,
Carved surgical instruments, salves
And unguents, knot-technique that verges
On lurid, and mumbled shifts
Of perception like the heated glass twisting
Above sand into a fabulous creature,
Replete with armoury sharps;
Would have led them to believe
What preceded yours and still receives
Your mind, dispersed in time, as matrix,
As disease, quite unsurprised, might perceive
Its aetiology—that is, unnecessary.
A column of dried flowers, pallid,
Lightly turns from the beams.
Both the column of dead furbelows
And the beams are placed, being recent,
To assist in orientation to the ancient.
They will deteriorate, in being recent,
As the robed figures in the wilderness
Must have; they will etiolate, etiolate,

And vanish outright, and the lace-lines
In the wings of the sketches of insects
Three thousand years old, vivid, and
Their static in summer, after all,
Like print.

AS WAS

I did not mind my life. For years
I squatted in the market, just past
the stall of bright silks, half-naked
in the soot and flame, and banged
brass to a bright roil, heard
the bubble of solder, hiss
of orange-tipped iron in water,
and drew the kufic letters of His name
in soft copper with a nail
on long-handled coffeepots.
At some point, I became a man.

The customers told me of
the various worlds, ocean storms
and doldrums, the sunken
brainlike world of coral, of
poison seashells with the smoothest
whorls, the prettiest echelons of
sawtooth pattern, of maidens laughing
and splashing in jungle pools, where
crimson and mauve flicks of fish
dart under rocks, and in the hanging
canopy of vines, there, a black

tail slowly swishing, sleek
panther yawning in the birdsong,
mocked by monkeys, primitively *louche*
on a low branch, eyes burning
like gold in the pool below. Ibn Battuta
himself has not traveled as I have
in their narratives, and my hands
kept crafting as they talked,
the details of the work submerged
in motive, tongues always probing
for the obligation knotted decades down

the long rope ladder of my family;
their eyes dim twin entreaties
to be parleyed into gain, the words
polite and meaningless, the real subject
never surfacing, until auspicious.
I have lived so long with the oblique,
I can no longer say things straight.
At mealtimes I would stray
to the caravanserai, where came
the wanderers who needed more time
with the animals before entering

the human web. Whole husks of moons
they had been between waters. The animals'
eyes still held the strain of destination.
They'd loosen the leather and metal
riggings of the beasts, darkened by use
at the edges, crusty with salt-sweat.
The braided ropes, the fine-stitched
panniers, the smooth-grooved saddles.
They fell in the dust in liberations.
There was a time when you could tell
the provenance of each traveler

by their deliberate, blue-ridged scars,
their bracelets, tassels, pierced ears and lips,
the wood discs in their mouths,
the bead rings round and round their necks,
their signature robes and turbans.
Now everybody is from everywhere;
they climb in tee shirts, jeans and sunglasses
from their dusty jeeps, and troop past
the rows of concrete shells, the junked cars
and satellite dishes to the one hotel.
They stop; I flog my copper gadgets.

I did not mind my life, the noise, the flame,
the crooked fingers of an artisan, but in sum
it is the thin mist in the hollow of
a dream I've had, so that a haggler's tale
has as much substance as my own experience.
The beasts, they pawed the earth,
shook water, satisfied, from their jowls.
The dark-faced men with rifles cross their laps.
My family, how track their slow diaspora?
In my workshop sand blows in triangular
dunes in the corners, in which I stick

the reproachful, angular black hulks
of abandoned projects, metal untransformed.
At least, at last, the clouds and darkening hills
are sweet instances of how He, insinuator,
penetrator, sole divisor, has lent shape
from shadow from His generosity, makes
stones swim underground and falcons
plummet, made the shifting gift
of water, and against the formless void
will have sketched the constellations.
The wind is more and more insistent.

ACKNOWLEDGEMENTS

Poems from *Morbidity and Ornament* first appeared in:

The Antigonish Review
CV2
Dream Catcher (UK)
Event
The Fiddlehead
Geist
Grain
The Malahat Review
Queen's Quarterly
Vallum
The Literary Review of Canada

Thanks to the editors of these journals, and to Catherine Greenwood, Catherine Owen, Steve McOrmond, Richard King, Shao Meng Lu, Patricia and Terence Young, Michael and Lynn Borich and Qu Fang Li for their encouragement; and to The Canada Council for financial support.

A line in "Cigarette Humors" owes something to a poem by Derk Wynand in *One Cook, Once Dreaming*. "Aquino" refers to passages in "Seebe", by Erin Mouré, and *The Ice Age*, by Rick Moody. "Blossoms of Chang'an," alludes to a Tang Dynasty poem entitled "Successful at the Civil Service Examinations," by Ming Jiao. "Meanwhile Evidence of Admiral Zheng He's..." takes off from information in *1421: The Year the Chinese Discovered The World*, by Gavin Menzies, which speculates about 15th century Chinese landings in North America.

The Chinese poems are my own fault, but I must give credit to UBC's Mandarin Proficiency Test Office for providing a scholarship to study in Shanghai in the summer of 2006.